T0083678

VENTIFACTS

VENTIFACTS

CHRISTINE HUME

OMNIDAWN PUBLISHING
RICHMOND, CALIFORNIA
2012

Cover photo: Map of Wind over Pacific Ocean
Courtesy: NASA / Photo Researchers, Inc.,
307 Fifth Avenue, Third Floor, New York, NY 10016,
http://www.photoresearchers.com

Description: Satellite map of wind speed and direction over the
Pacific Ocean. The arrows represent wind direction and the colors
wind speed. Blue indicates wind speeds of 0-14 kilometres per hour (kph),
purple and pink speeds of 15-43 kph, red and orange speeds of 44-72 kph.
The image was derived from data obtained on 14 September 1978 by the
scatterometer instrument on NASA's Seasat satellite.

Cover and Interior Design by Cassandra Smith

Typefaces: Bell Gothic Std and Adobe Caslon Pro

Printed on Finch 60# Recycled 30% PCW Natural Opaque Vellum

Published by Omnidawn Publishing, Richmond, California
www.omnidawn.com   (510) 237-5472   (800) 792-4957
10 9 8 7 6 5 4 3 2 1
978-1-890650-65-0

Thanks to the *Seneca Review* for publishing an early version of *Ventifacts*.

Thanks also to Amy Kulper, whose mental weathers inspire.

The sounds we don't recognize flying out of our huge mouths: curses of the furies, songs of the sirens, the babblings of Cassandra, all those horrifying sounds burbling up from a female body. The dreadful groan of the Gorgon sisters, whose name derives from the Sanskrit *garg* (think gargle or gag), a guttural animal wail that issues a great wind from the back of the throat. Through a pendulous mouth, time itself howls.

Literally, a ventifact is a "wind artifact."

To distinguish them from gizzard stones or yardangs, [1] know that ventifacts are the abrasions, etchings, flutes, pits, grooves, facets, and polishings on wind-blasted stones. These morphologies indicate current wind conditions; they texture the present with paleo-patterns, winds from well before we were born.

In the flattest places, wind blows between my daughter's second and third year. It is her year of fighting whatever's fleeting. Her year of convection in mysterious tributaries. Leaving babyhood for childhood knocks the wind out of her *and* gives her a second wind that reanimates the elemental, re-rigging experience through newly organized senses. Yet to control sensation is to betray it. We come to view all her exhalations as potential screams. All this happens below the moon. We process wind in pulses.

A windy tree tempts her to devote herself to interstices, to partake in its shadowtackle. She climbs up to disappear. She climbs through trembling leaves and their inaudible decibels. She is a microphone held up to a tree. She would do anything not to hear it, to keep herself wrapped in dreaming, were it not for that tiny pinch of bitter joy that draws her. Alone, wind-drawn, withdrawn, she knows the only way out is on a gust. What is the wind passing from tree to tree? In an oceanic rush, leaves cast around their seedy eyes. Its static devours a sleeping pink rabbit. Shivelight roars through her, releasing the joy that's been petrified, dark, and furtive. This joy is the main thing. Yet as soon as it rushes in, fear washes over it: they take turns with her. Those chapters of joy and fear keep turning, and then suddenly in spite of it all, she has expectations.

In Nietzsche's "weather prophets," wind tells us nothing but *the now* as seen through *then*: "Just as the clouds tell us the direction of the wind high above our heads, so the lightest and freest spirits are in their tendencies foretellers of the weather that is coming. The wind in the valley and the opinions of the market-place of today indicating nothing of that which is coming but only of that which has been."[2] Wind brings us the future we were trained for.

Wind is a tiny prospect, an active mimetic force working expressly inside things. Wind never disappears, it goes into remission. When there is no wind, there is breeze; there is draft, nascent stirrings, and ominous stillness. Because we live on a rotating planet with fire and ice, the very air brings the threat of wind. It carries anguished assassins. Anyone who is attuned to air knows to look for its tracings and ransoms.

We look out the window at blue sky cut with a vapor trail, the specter of a plane on the way to Detroit. Up there is filled with my daughter's gleaned idea of heaven, teeming with transitive ghosts and eternal spirits. With their swift operations and transmitting talents, winds have often been taken for angels. An uplifting power is their second nature. The child breathes that evanescence into the world. It reminds her of how powerful she is, how epic, how exhausted.

She stops, shudders, and runs back for the door. It's finally spring and she refuses to go outside. I have no idea how to help her; she's not yet three, gripping my leg. Wind where an ocean had been. Shifting and peaking. Someone puts a rock in her palm to help her feel fiercely unmoved. With large animals, she's brave; in the dark, she's unfazed. But wherever the wind touches her, she grows raw nerve. Skin is a field of nerves where wind had been. She holds her hat to her head even after we get in the car and all the way to the store: *I saw an ant fight wind. They were fighting together over the pigeon's toy.* She points out flags and balloons batting around on used car lots. All the branches tack out of time. All the pines bend toward the highway. In the store, she palms the rock and shouts at strangers, *I'm not afraid of you wind!* Their faces drifting by on dead air.

We breathe a military climatology, it's the leitmotif of terrorism. Instead of traditional body-to-body combat, we re-design, re-assign, resign the air. Designing killer environments for our enemies consolidates the most salient givens of our world: terrorism, design consciousness, and environmental thinking.[3] That's the setting, but how to get the story going? Try this: what's in the wind? Was it speaking, or chasing someone, or on a mission, or asleep? When German soldiers released chlorine gas into a north by northwest wind on April 22, 1915 in Northern France, which way the wind was blowing meant your ass.

In 1996 the US Department of Defense issued a now-infamous paper, "Weather as a Force Multiplier: Owning the Weather in 2025," which hypothesizes ways in which weather modification technologies might give the US a "weather edge" over potential adversaries.[4] It does so through "fictionalized representations of future scenarios" involving weaponized weather. Imagine, it asks us, the US fighting a powerful drug cartel in South America by controlling the target area meteorologically. By engineering wind flow patterns—an air theater, a perfectly orchestrated wind opera—we can engineer vulnerability. We'll make them weep and weak. With chemical interventions that would withhold precipitation to induce drought, then unleash catastrophic storms, flash flooding, or climate shifts, the US military sneaks in disguised as an act of nature. This is a repeatable story. A pilot project conducted in 1966 artificially extended the monsoon season along the Ho Chi Minh trail by releasing silver iodide, a hazardous, toxic pollutant that stopped people in their tracks. Big winds and heavy rainfall wreaked havoc on the land, inhibiting human movement, and the chemical agent made people fall sick. Since 1993, a research station in Gakona, Alaska has been practicing various means of ionospheric control.[5] The ionosphere is the ceiling of the atmosphere, a no-man's land between the atmosphere and the magnetosphere. In this transitional space, the Ionospheric Research Instrument blasts high-powered radio waves in a single beam with 180 antennas in order to take down aircraft, manipulate wind and set off calamities, nature made-to-order. This research station, the High Frequency Active Auroral Research Program or HAARP, as its commonly acronymized, waits for its story to materialize in the security domains, as canards and conspiracy talk squall under the radio waves. This world is HAARP's testing ground. All of this makes Mahmoud Ahmadinejad's claim that Europe is stealing Iran's rain, emptying their clouds before the clouds wind-travel to the East—reported widely in the conservative press in May 2011—seem not only feasible, but probable. A gust of absolute conviction, prescient announcement, and paranoia sometimes blow through the same moment.

At one point in Henry Darger's *Conflagration!* the Vivian girls find themselves trapped by a forest fire set by the Glandelinians: "It appeared to be a fire storm of a sixty-mile-an-hour velocity, by the way it swept the trees down in so great a number, the wind coming straight from the southwest raging with the most terrible fury." But the wind eventually changes course and so changes the state of affairs, a fury turned back to where it began.

In the parking lot, sleepless stones skim the asphalt, each one its own double. A thing in wind is caffeinated, buzzing with aura. Rustling newspaper wrapped around nothing. Wind animates empties. Loose plastic bags derange into amoeba-puppets hopping around parked cars. Marks of visitation, marks of limbo. Open asphalt is a habitat for loose shopping carts, kinetic water bottles, newspaper pages, and sea gulls trolling for trash. Wind rustles the tissue wrapped around each thing. A giddy piece of time translates you, too. Whoever wants to inflate, to be carried away, to turn tail, to come skidding back, to change and exchange is susceptible to the wind: *take me with you, away from forsaken here.*

In Portugal, according to Pliny the Elder, wind-foals could get you there. When the winds came, mares set their tails against it and conceived by "that genital air instead of natural seed." In time they gave birth to "foals as swift as the wind," who never lived longer than three years.[6] This is a literal second wind, a brief rush before taking leave. A joke might begin: what do a second wind and love have in common?

Wind arouses amorphously, omnisciently. It excites water, skims the skin in little slanting waves. Whatever the sun intensifies, whenever it boils, the wind comes along as its ecstatic relief. Wind is sun cum. Spewing seeds, debris and rays. It is all tentacles, all jellyfish experience; a weathervane theater with hooks and stays.

As sudden as headlights reeling through dark windows, the squall delivers its scream. Comes so loud that the sun's burning cannot be heard. Slams shut my trap, the wind shuts, it seizes, disfigures words, pelts the glass with red pebbles. Wind deals me its ordeal of airs, pushes on the spot, says *decide* amidst the shouting and thundering, skin all gooseflesh, dress billowing, my womb floats out, hangs like a threatening cloud. It grows ears and listens. The infant wind kicks, it sucks whatever sticks out, unzips and zips switches, teethes on skin. Won't be stuck in a blowout. Won't stop grabbing my red ears, it rattles my ribcage. The ear is the last face, and the wind puts distance in it.

Up close, its helmet of harsh vowels whispers too close to decipher; from the other side of the field, its rustle beckons, sometimes lifts into a zeroing whistle. And sometimes, its glossolalic hush multiplies the possibilities of speech. Yet in the forests of linguistic semblance, wind becomes a vocalization of whoever hears it.

Coming at her from every direction, wind is her private terrorist threatening body, home, and family with a huff and a puff. She looks for a place to hide. Wind exposes and inflates instabilities. When she's in it, she thinks the world makes her flinch. What will it blow away today? What has been accounted for? All things are equal exchange for wind, and we have lost her to the bargain.

Admit it, wind is a pathetic stand-in for spirit or soul, a god, a hungry ghost, a demon, a germ. An image stops time, but wind emphasizes its relentless continuing.

A wind might carry an epidemic disease from infected place to clean place, or poisons of low-lying lands and slums might migrate into middle class neighborhoods. These notions haunted Britain from the turn of the nineteenth century until germ theory gained esteem three quarters of a century later. In those times, wind agitated the mind and disturbed the body. In the midst of the 1848 national cholera epidemic, during the formation of England's first General Board of Health, while her siblings, one by one, slid from illness into death, during the time of writing of her social problem novel, *Shirley*, Charlotte Brontë's letters blame the return of fever to "this cruel east wind," "cold penetrating wind," "wind blowing," and "frost and east wind."[7] In *Shirley*, which takes the Luddite uprisings in the Yorkshire textile industry as its backdrop, Caroline, rendered vulnerable by "mental excitement" and "habitual sadness," falls prey to "some sweet, poisoned breeze, redolent of honey-dew and miasma" passing through her "lungs and veins" on her walk home from Hollow's cottage. Wind medicalizes place in Brontë's novel. If deleterious winds can ultimately transform a healthy place to a sick one, they can also tell the future: "winds commissioned to bring in fog the yellow taint of pestilence, covering white Western isles with the poisoned exhalations of the East, dimming the lattice of English homes with the breath of Indian plague."[8] These racist associations of miasma with

Asia and the East were commonplace at the time; for instance, one harbormaster's account attributes a cholera outbreak to a hot breeze "with a bog-like smell, passing from the East over them."[9] Sailors in mid-nineteenth-century England sometimes outfitted their sails with special apparatuses to filter "the African atmosphere, as a cook strains calf's-foot jelly."[10] The nomenclature of English imperialism is absolutely to the point: Brontë's depiction of plague comes in racial terms—the "*yellow* taint of pestilence" infects the "*white* Western isles"—as well as meteorological terms to establish an atmosphere and location of ideology. Xenophobia induced a fear of wind, which is a fear of borderlessness.

In the next chapter, "West Wind Blows," our cholera-tinted protagonist is wind-corrected:

> So long as the breath of Asiatic deserts parched Caroline's lips and fevered her veins, her physical convalescence could not keep pace with her returning mental tranquility; but there came a day when the wind ceased to sob at the eastern gable of the Rectory, and at the oriel window of the church. A little cloud like a man's hand arose in the west; gusts from the same quarter drove it on and spread it wide; wet and tempest prevailed a while. When that was over the sun broke out genially, heaven regained its azure, and the earth its green: the livid cholera-tint had vanished from the face of nature: the hill rose clear round the horizon, absolved from that pale malaria haze.

Wind plays on the mind because it harbors a history of toxic acts, its taint of its past lives. The place a wind begins creates its character. Picture what the air's full of—truck exhaust, ragweed pollen, garlic smell, shortwave signals, hash smoke, germs of the coming plague—as mean-faced demons invisible to the naked eye. Whole populations of pollution and purity. Though Greeks often drew the wind gods as galloping horses or as lithe winged humans, the Greek god Boreal emerged as a burly man with exaggerated facial features and a rack of wild hair. Often he holds a windbag in his hands. This god's iconography swept along the Silk Road finally transmuting into the Shinto wind god Fujin.[11]

Conversely, Aristotle believed "every wind is weakest in the spot from which it blows," an anti-origins stance that advocates gaining power through experience: as winds "proceed from their source at a distance, they gather strength."[12] If the wind itself is divine, a common belief in Aristotle's time, it becomes so through eternal motion and is not born that way. In this view, a fully active life might beget holy status, not monkish abnegation, not a stilled mind, not divine right.

In his 1988 memoir, *The Wind Spirit*, Michel Tournier sees astral winds living at human pace: "A cloud forms in the sky like an image in my brain, the wind blows like I breathe...." Wind constitutes an implicit condition of existence where a stirred latency—whatever had been unrealized, unthought, unperceived—awakes. And as a catalyst to consciousness, every waking sensation inducts its own rhythm. Perhaps these correspond in a kind of scale—like Beaufort's—based on empirical experience. According to Beaufort, we know a near gale over water by the way the sea "heaps up," and foam from breaking waves streak in the wind's direction. On land we see "whole trees in motion. Effort needed to walk against the wind. Swaying of skyscrapers may be felt, especially by people on the upper floors."[13] Writing this reminds me that before scientists kept it captive, before language narrativized it, wind quickened hearts, flexed an originary joy.

It used to be the realm of the ancient gods, but now our weather reports reflect regional ontologies. They structure our collective psyche; to describe wind is to attempt to supply the senses with a recognizable narrative. Even my windowsill weather forecaster depicts wind as a series of straight lines pushing into a cloud. It's hard not to see a tree uprooted and turned on its side, the billowing canopy rendered in a child's shorthand. It seems to say, this too will end badly. Like the speed lines in comics, inspired by mathematical vectors used to indicate direction and strength, and from long-exposure photography that smears light in the direction of motion, wind-lines make our very air visible, reminding us of our dependence on it. What do we resent more than a dependence we did not choose, one that mocks our dear individuality, our commitment to the singularity of our own stories?

My daughter's voice pours like red and white from the icy divide: *Once when I was tiny the wind carried me to its river; I was its ghost because I turned everything you said back. I was its shadow then and wrapped myself around you. The ghost was information.* Her voice slurs when she speaks through wind. And when she looks through it, as hardly she ever does, she sees tingling between dusk and silver. If she can find the still spot, she is in the divine eye:

(Aeolus, Africus, Amaunet, Anzu, Aquilo, Arar Tiotio, Aura, Auster, Ays, Bacabs, Boreas, Bucca, Buluga, Bunzi, Chaob, Chi Po, Chup, Coatrischie, Corus, Dagoda, Dagwanoenyent, Dajoji, Ecalochot, Egoi, Ehecatl, Ellil, El Nuberu, Enlil, Eurus, Fa'atiu, Favonius, Fae Lian, Fengbo, Feng-Po-Po, Fisaga, Fongshihye, Fujin, Ga-Oh, Guabancex, Ha'hl'tunk'ya, Hanui-o-Rangi, Hau, Haya-Ji, Hermes, Hine-Tu-Whenua, Hotoru, Hraesvelg, Hurakan, Ilmarinen, Kabun, Kaikias, Kami-kaze, Kon, Kukulcan, La'a Maomao, Mamacocha, Mari, Matagi, Mata Upola, Matuu, Mbon, Michabo, Neoga, Ninlil, Ninurta, Njord, Notus, Óloma, Oonawieh Unggi, Oya, Paka'a, Pan-gu, Quetzalcoatl, Raja Angin, Rudra, Saíshiwani, Saúshuluma, Shine-Tsu-Hiko, Shu, Shutu, Skeiron, Stribog, Susanowa, Szélkirály, Tamats, Tate, Tonga, Tsailútsanok'ka, Tua-Uo-Loa, Twhiri, Tempestates, Unáhsinte, Vatam Vayu, Venti, Ventolines,

Vila, Vulturnus, Wabun, Wakwiyo, Yansan, Ya-o-gah, Yondung Halmoni, Yu Ch'iang, Zephyros)

She's inside that animal, the body of a cosmic animal with a stellar eye. Speak, transparence! Listen to the little girl singing in the wind pit—the echo distorts her phrases. Wind smears her voice, serrates its edges. She is sustained, infused, captivated by its mixed airs. She will live through its illusion.

Try to file the wind's incarnations away neatly in the alphabet. Subject it to lists, taxonomies, archives. Try and try to house it, but wind will not be ordered or efficient. It won't be accounted for. Not structured around human senses. Not serialized.

From "wind" comes "wing," or they share a root in "to blow." Due to the influence of "windy," pronunciation of "wind" shifts to a short vowel in the eighteenth century. Before this it rhymed with mind. On wing or in mind, away we go. For Bachelard, flight exceeds its forms and vehicles: wind forms the bird even as it effaces the bird in flight.[14] Now what does wind rhyme with? Sinned? Thinned? Pinned? Moving like eyes reading text on the page, wind lurches, it back-pedals, it digresses endlessly. What at first seems steady and direct is riddled with re-direction.

All winter she has been immune, over-bundled, cloistered past sensation. Now her bare arms and legs prickle electric. She tries to run from the feeling. Runs across the empty baseball field, crying. Away from the wind on her skin. She tries, crying and hearing a roar of nothing. Sometimes it's still like that—fleeting and loaded. When I am running with the kite, it looks like I'm with the wind bolting away from her. But I hold my breath until, *see*, I shout and point skyward. She is running and crying. *Look*, I say, *look* as our blue kite lifts into the clear blue. It is difficult to approach the beyond in a good mood. Wind knows dispiriting voids. Its source is hidden, like a human's. The kite string snaps for the third time. She wants to go home, and is afraid of being blown home, or of the story blowing away again.

Way ahead flags slacken, then a bleeder goes by, a crazed galactic blast elides with green skies. When air is locked in a moon-pocket, a sudden bird might rip it open and pilot a storm. We station ourselves around town—connected and concealed by its thousand white horses and forty-nine purple horses, and arrows from Arjuna. Wind's frontiers proliferate. Here's one now: one of us tries to swallow it; one of us tries to lure it into her bottle; another keeps shoving it down a big crack in the black rock. When yardangs—wind-sculpted land—start rearing up, everyone stops in their tracks and sees sphinxes.

Wanderer, where are you?

Beyond the wind, Herodotus and Pliny describe, is Hyperborea where people live in complete happiness for a very long time. I imagine this place suffocating rage, uncertainty, hangdog blues—the ways in which I know myself. Whole emotional lives snuffed out. In windlessness lies our last chance of self-erasing.

In the world of childhood, wind is a mystifying agent, a sonic wish passed from parent to child. As the children sit by the fire deep in the woods waiting for their parents to return, they listen to the strokes of their father's axe cutting firewood. They believe he is near, working for their comfort, and under the spell of this soporific rhythm, they fall asleep. Firelight dances on their blank eyelids. Yet, "it was not the axe, but a branch which he had fastened to a withered tree which the wind was blowing backwards and forwards." Once deceived by the wind, they try the same trick on the witch. When the witch first speaks—

> "Nibble, nibble, gnaw,
>
> Who is nibbling at my little house?"

—the children answer:

> "The wind, the wind,
>
> The heaven-born wind."[15]

But the witch, having a bat's eyesight and a nose as good as a dog's, has smelled them coming. And, of course, it's not the same trick, for the wind never announces itself; it allows listeners to fool themselves. The children have confused sign and signifier in their attempt at shape-shifting. They must after all feel invisible as wind—abandoned by their parents, starving, lost—and at the same time, they might be sending out a kind of invocation. But the "heaven-born wind" does not save them, they must save themselves.

Is it sadistic not to shelter my daughter? Not to validate the experience of her own feelings? Am I squelching the power of her interior life by rejecting its vivid manifestations? Am I enabling her to develop the wisdom of not believing everything she thinks?

I'm in line at the grocery store about ten days after Japan's massive earthquake-induced nuclear reactor leakage. I have heard Yukio Edano, Japan's chief cabinet secretary's words, "With evacuation in place and the ocean-bound wind, we can ensure safety,"[16] but I can't say I put any stock in them. The woman in front of me puts a white bottle on the conveyor belt: "Potassium iodide," she volunteers, "protects the thyroid from radiation." We are both staring at the bottle as she adds, "I heard it on the radio; a recent ocean wind brought it here. The radiation is just now hitting Michigan."

Take the shape of music: chimes, bells, Aeolian harp, the natural minor key. All the rushes whisper at once when the wind blows through. Wind is the first music, a soundscape for an ecosystem. Take the shape of a giddy piece of time, and keeping time, cattails interpret the language of the wind (not the wind), which gets itself into the clock. As Laura Riding gets out, "Every minute for itself."[17]

Take the shapes of language: whirl, helix, sheet, and zigzag. The whirl is where the horizon cannot be remembered. The helix sends you up in a war column, surrounded by turkey buzzards chasing tail. The sheet interred you once; next time it comes, you will build a raft. This wind's cursed genius is to control the tension of your longing. Its exorbitant body updrafts, its heart beats faster than we can hear. The zigzag synchronizes like an audience clapping. It cannot go on like this.

Anyone who has ever stared too long into the wind waiting for someone to come through knows: It cannot go on like this.

Anticipation—dread—makes her cower at the merest stirrings, and I seize up knowing what comes next: her diva-level belting out against it. In this instant my face mirrors hers: her shriek echoes the wind. We are analogies hoping to lead ourselves out of passivity. Yet in the land of troubles, every wind is the same. Wind makes us both too permeable and too solid. It pushes us around, it makes us mistake our bodies for water or dirt. And empathy can make you susceptible. When Mark Epstein's three-year-old developed a pronounced fear of wind, he writes, "we went out of our way to reassure her and shield her, but her fear only grew more intense, and my wife and I began to react with a start ourselves whenever a breeze came up."[18] If I could hold up a mirror to her: but no child can recognize her own terrorizer staring back at her. *The invisibility and intangibility of that which moves us remains unfathomable.*[19]

Lay down beneath the windmills in your life. Sleep in a field of turbines, each over a hundred feet tall, three blades *that's the way* going around *uh huh uh huh* in threes *I like it*. The mills act with one mind to summon the power of love. Wait for the wind to carry you head over heels. Braiding horses' breath and breaking smoke on the blades. Nine airs lash into one signal. The blades turn. Memories and predictions spin, uncoiling new forms and figures. Recall what it felt like to wait on the verge of voice, on the edge of sex. Wind rushes over, always incomplete. Can't you ever quite enter, can't you come to? Make a wish on a turbine. Dream of being weightless. Ask the sky to suspend you. Your memory of flight comes with a confidence that you will be able to levitate. At least, for a split second, you will sail. But it doesn't take you. You are not swept away. Wind does not make events move faster, nor does it turn speech into song, but it can translate a lapse. Voices run through *that's the way* if a word clings there, it is remembering *uh huh uh huh*. What did you say? Wind's voice must never be let loose, no matter how close to sleep you creep.

Its true wailings are mythical lustrations. Wind is a noisy flock that mosquitoes ride and bite. Wind is an animal born of space. A low one can be taken for a snake; a forested one can be taken for a witch. We are all this animal once a day, this wind. Tongue like a bell, an alarming chorus of planes, sirens, lawn mowers, barking dogs in every direction.

"The thin dog is running in the road, this dog is the road." It barks as I read Virginia Woolf. Bark: this writing is wind. It is etherializing the former precision and authority of its sources. Bark: the dog chases it down. The road barks and growls at the wind. Follow it to where a child is running between articulate speech and meaningless voices. This writing is pissing in the wind.

The tormented skies of J.M.W. Turner's paintings rub out details in favor of pure color and motion, shreds of horizon outgassing the sublime. External weathers compete with internal ones. To some critics, Turner's Romanticism suggests civic disengagement and escapism. But rather than retreating into landscape, Turner fully acknowledged the complexity of England's newly hybridized industry-and-nature. In his work, the local effects of weather are interrogated by and infused with the larger scale and aggregated duration of "climate," a rethinking of our very relationship with environment. In fact, the paintings that immortalized the Yorkshire Dales rely so tangibly on moving atmospherics that they almost anticipate the two industrial wind turbines planned next year for Bolton Abbey. The paintings made firmament enough for another appropriation, another kind of ruin, another transformative potency.

My child points her finger accusingly at what the mind might displace: shovel, Echinacea petals, compost pile, color of everything painted. Things hold their own longing to self-destruct, to be lost or disappeared. She wants to be sure I stay. She fixates on the missing ball. Imagines its pleasure in rolling away. Dandelions gone to seed send out the wish for their former lives. To roll back, to skid back under the radar, under the semiotic bar. If I rolled away to a time before she was born. Would that hold the pleasure I imagine it would, that I can now only imagine?

When I was pregnant I sat on a wind farm listening and dividing. Divining and deciding: I would not be party to a hermetic cycle, a doomed family. I would tap a new source, and become less responsible for my token selves. Dividing and undecided, I sat under turbines; a coin kept turning. Rotary and helical winds combined into feedback loops and propelled electromagnetism in spirals. We report wind by the direction from which it originates. Start again: horizon-and-sun whorl in the eye. The fulcrum uplifts and twists, catching me in a rhythmic mote of questioning. Its yes-or-no rhythm opposes any instant of relief. Around and round rhythms lay down words among the straying planets. Wind is a circulatory system with cybernetic steering. The eye's inverse-wind draws things to it, even the newest ear sucks down whatever it can. In utero an ear forms and functions at sixteen weeks—long before the genitalia forms or the eyes function. The curl re-integrates light and sound.

Or the earsplitting whirl of blades and their "shadow flicker," cutting through the sun into midnight in mechanized beats, might over-carbonate your mind. When I want strobe and unrelenting loudness, I'll know where to go. But when no one's around, the turbines can create miniature Edens under their motherly arms. The steady, gentle turbulence they create makes for more than good enough crops. [20]

When no one's around, what is wind? Is it just one more feral thing in the wilderness? In the nineteenth century, as a phantom of sublimity and carrier of death, wind was an accomplice to will. Didn't we all used to be like the wind, pure and strong, stroking the strings of imagination, blowing open vowels through a flute? Didn't we all wish someone would die? The woods resounded with weather or weaponry. In the twenty-first century, we wax nostalgic for winds with location and context, for an unglobalized gust, for an unpasteurized pastoral breeze in which submersion becomes a form of companionship, an encounter with an other, an inspiration.

Does this weather narrative begin with a character? We name storms after women[21]— impulsive, angry, retaliatory, demanding, loud, shifty, destructive forces—in an inscription of ideology so complete that it took until 1979, seven years after Title IX, to change it.

Or our girl with the pipes is afraid of wind claiming her name.

Furred wind carrying unctuous tongues.

Southern anabatic winds sand-pelting the eyes.

Permanent winds that never bloom.

A three-day wind out of California spitting ecstasy on the skin.

A secret blast startles the grackles.

White wind throwing stones at statues.

In red wind, windmills sharpen.

Typhoons that repeatedly deter or enable armies to attack.

Smells on the wind like music, a premonition that you won't come back.

A daughter declared war on the wind.

Once the officials sent a poison wind to her country as a warning. She became wind-drunk in minutes. She became a surprised spectator, dizzied with alien energy. Anticlockwise wind rewinds a lone delight. Then the entire ground was inches thick in petals and pollen, breaking her fall.

She runs out on the balcony to catch wind in her hands. She runs back in to sic the wind on me, throwing it into my face from her tight fists. In a mood to court suffering, her fingers have veins that go right to the heart. She means it as she thrusts poison windflowers on me and turns, runs out again for more. She is trying to inflict pain, to set anguish upon my face. Mama-blowout in a dissolving cloak, mother of atrophied arms and evacuating lap, mother-tongue lashing or torn out. This outburst is shaped and sharpened by wind, which is speaking through her. It hits me and splatters, wind-grit abrades walls, leaving rock varnish—dark, shiny stains—as it creates deflation zones. Over a dozen times she comes at me with fists full of wind. Its projectile impulse is a spell pouring over us; it convulses us in pleasure, chafes us, blizzards a dull melancholy. In her hands, she is holding and releasing me.

To bring the sound of wind inside is to invite the eeriest waftings of vulnerability.

But a thick, vertiginous curtain of glass shuts out an auditory outside. Look out the sealed window to a dynamic cityscape below. This visual vitality is so colorful, so kinetic, and so out of sync with its sonic deadness, it nauseates. For his *World Trade Center Recordings* (1999/2001), Stephen Vitiello stuck contact mics to the windows to convert one of the world's tallest buildings into a monumental microphone. With these recordings, we listen to what no human had heard before: severe winds outside the 91st floor of one tower, suddenly audible like a mystic thought thrashing around a steel brain.

Visually saturated, I stumble into a museum room where one piece from this series, *Winds After Hurricane Floyd*, plays in a darkened room. Nothing in the room but white vinyl seats and the sound of an end-of-the-century hurricane raging outside a building that no longer exists. This is what the new century remembers of the old. What the WTC offered us was a graphic majesty that strangled all sound; what we have now is an aural memory basking in the aura of recently departed visuals. What is left of the WTC is the sound of its sweeping winds, what it stood in the way of. The building creaking its tiny resistance.

Listening out, if we'd only listened to the ghostly charge of these recordings earlier, we would have heard our own fragility. I am hearing it now, searingly clear. Another queasy disparity asserts itself: the sound of "nothing" has architectural gravitas. The winds surge and drone, no stories in sight.

Purity isn't a matter of separation—she could never see herself dissolved into wind or melted out of it. Her terror contains a more intensive contamination. What would wind find in her? Would it find her empty enough to inflate? Full enough to extinguish? When a wind bloom snuffs a candle, a new eye is born. It is an eye that doesn't open, it lets her stay inside it. Yet a wind prescription might soften the edges of things. It might ripen eyes, or cure them as was once believed. A wind-eye, from the Old Norse *vindr* and *auga*, is the origin of "window." To see clearly, note the frame. Websters' 1828 Dictionary tell us the vulgar pronunciation is "windor," as if from the Welsh *gwyntdor*, wind-door.

Wind portal: But how can you soften what you can't see? At a distance, you can't tell which way the windmill rotates. A kinetic depth magic called the "Windmill Illusion" won't let you equivocate. Your mind decides involuntarily, it doesn't like facing the noncommittal nature of speed. Doesn't want to recognize air's variability.

Wind portal: Failed or stalled wind projects stud the coastline like shipwrecks—CapeWind, Bluewater Wind, Padre Island, Long Time. While the offshore wind industry searches for its clinching narrative—it harvests, harnesses, mines, taps, or traffics pure energy?—a suspicion in what we can't see digs itself in. Why not strap a bridle on god? Would windmills become worshipped icons? What if I need that air to breathe?

Wind Portal: The first sculptures were made by wind, polished like glass in some surfaces, jagged in others; formations of on-going memory. The very first drawings may have been of wind. Grasses making impressions, stone tracks in sand. Nineteenth century paintings of moving mists, steam, smoke, and fog remind us of wind's picturesque, sublime, and tragic powers. The need has always been with us: to perceive the imperceptible. It hangs over us like a new law, a threat. Or a dare: who can tame the generative abundance and clarifying infinitude of wind?

Jeff Wall's *A Sudden Gust of Wind (after Hokusai)* depicts an odd assortment of wind-startled city and country characters, played by amateur actors: two men clutching hats to their heads, while a third stares up in the sky at his hat; a woman with a scarf blown over her face by the same gust that has sent her sheets of paper flying into the air, mingling with dead leaves from two trees that bend in the direction of the wind. This design is scrupulously appropriated—the particular torque of the characters' bodies to the fractal patterns of escaping sheets of paper and dead leaves—from one of Katsushika

Hokusai's *Thirty-six Views of Mount Fuji* (1831–33). Wall reanimates a wind from nineteenth century Japan, directing it to a contemporary cranberry bog in Canada. The ultimate force of unpredictability and havoc here carefully repeats its earlier effects. Wall's wind doesn't duplicate, however, Hokusai's mountain, his nominal subject matter, and the absence is blaring. What jumps into its void is the sheer scale of Wall's piece. By rendering his picture twelve times as large as the original, the mountainousness remains. Another way of looking at it is that Wall reveals wind as the true subject. Refusing to give the wind a backboard (that is, the mountain), Wall lets the viewer's eye overwhelm with the vastness of unobstructed sky. The wind takes on the majesty and power of the mountain directly; the metaphor has dropped its referent, the essence of which has been fully absorbed into the vehicle.

In the perfection of nature and gesture, Wall composed his piece digitally out of over a hundred single shots.[22] It's actually a meticulous montage made to capture a sense of the precarious instant, the decisive moment. At the same time, it re-enacts an historical subject. These seemingly incompatible temporalities imbue the single photo with a sense of the cinema. Every frame stratifies subliminal effect. The iconography of wind translates spaces into powerful fictions and futures.

Wind portal: we stage our reactions. Our daughter's outrageous outbursts make us hold our breath. We contort and huddle against her shatteringly uncontainable squalls. One of us with hands over our ears, one of our faces turns to stone. The sky is both trembling and terrifying in this family portrait.

When we do finally launch the kite, she calls it a piñata. She watches it being battered about, jerking violently in all directions. We do not see the wind, we see what it gives rise to. Its palpable punch and drag is thrilling to watch. Run into the wind, I urge her—but she is not moving. Despite the kite's agility and occasional grace, the spectacle identifies her helplessness. She waits for candy to fall. She waits for *what* to fall from the howling torn mouth.

I wrote the letters in black marker on her knuckles, saying, would you like me to tell you the story of Right Hand and Left Hand—the story of move and rest? Now watch and I'll show you the story of life. R-E-S-T: It was with this left hand that brother struck the blow that laid his sister low. M-O-V-E: The right hand, the hand of move. These sister fingers are full of flow, on the go. The hands are always wrestling one another. When the fingers intertwine, a secret law unlocks. Now watch them. Brother Left Hand is fighting. And it looks like MOVE's a goner. But wait a minute, MOVE comes back on the break, Sister Right shows us what she's made of. It's MOVE that won, and REST is down for the count.[23]

HEAT and COLD are the parents of MOVE; repeat the above story with them as the actors in a pyrrhic victory. We think we see opposites instead of transitions. We think we see countless undulations, twistings, breakings instead of hands.

"We can tell whether we are happy by the sound of the wind. It warns the unhappy man of the fragility of his house, hounding him from shallow sleep and violent dreams. To the happy man it is the song of his protectedness: its furious howling concedes that it has power over him no longer."[24]

Once it beats the earth bare of yesterday's creases, we forget the germs. Let go. Wind-mind contains vertigo. Memory launches itself into the future, flaunting forth on an air-built thoroughfare.[25] But wait, the reversal takes you back so far, you are looking straight ahead. In Chicago, the lake effect reminds us of a time before she was born, incomprehensible to her. All three of us are walking hand-in-hand to the lake. She immediately draws us to a future in which she is big and we are little. Wind is sibyl, carrying germs that will speak your future. Carrying off half-thoughts to the echo tunnel. To get to the lake, we walk through a series of air-channeling tunnels under Chicago highways. We pass through knots and streaming: "Cadillac" the tunnel says today, "lilac," "sad sack," "heart attack." In the beach sand, a man had written huge letters spelling out "FEED ME," but the words are almost entirely effaced by the time we arrive.

[1] Yardangs are aerodynamically streamlined formations of cohesive material such as bedrock or lacustrine muds formed by unidirectional wind erosion. Ventifacts are the wind-sculptings on the windward face of a rock. The former is more of a ridge, the latter is more of a texture.

[2] Friedrich Nietzsche, "The Wanderer and His Shadow," *Human, All Too Human*. R.J. Hollingdale, trans., New York: Cambridge UP, 1996 (391).

[3] This entire paragraph is indebted to Peter Sloterdijk, Terror From the Air, Amy Patton and Steve Corcoran, trans., Cambridge, MA: MIT Press, 2009 (9-10, 25).

[4] Col Tamzy J. House, Lt Col James B. Near, Jr., LTC William B. Shields, Maj Ronald J. Celentano, Maj David M. Husband, Maj Ann E. Mercer, Maj James E. Pugh, presented August 1996: csat.au.af.mil/2025/volume3/vol3ch15.pdf.

[5] HAARP (High Frequency Active Auroral Research Program) is jointly funded by the US Air Force, the US Navy, the University of Alaska, and the Defense Advanced Research Projects Agency (DARPA).

[6] Pliny the Elder, *Natural History of C. Plinius Secundus*, Philemon Holland, trans., London: Centaur Press, 1962 (95).

[7] Thomes James Wise, ed., *The Brontës: Their Lives, Friendships and Correspondence*, vols I, II, Philadelphia: Porcupine Press, 1980 (175, 266, 268, 295, 322).

[8] All passages from Charlotte Brontë, *Shirley*, New York: Oxford UP, 1981.

[9] "Epidemics," *Westminster Review* 1, 1824 (334).

[10] "Reid-Ventilation," *Quarterly Review* 77, 1845-6 (401).

[11] According to Wikipedia: "Silk Road Transmission of Art."

[12] Aristotle, *Meteorology*, 350 B.C.E, E.W. Webster, trans. Internet Classics Archive: classics@classics.mit.edu.

[13] Beaufort's complete scale: http://www.spc.noaa.gov/faq/tornado/beaufort.html.

[14] Gaston Bachelard, *Air and Dreams*, Edith and Fredrick Farell, trans. Dallas, TX: Dallas Institute of Humanities & Culture, 1988 (86).

[15] *The Complete Grimm's Fairy Tales*, Margaret Hunt and James Stern, trans., New York: Random House-Pantheon Books, 1972/1857 (88, 90).

[16] Terry Macalister, Fiona Harvey, John Vidal and Justin McCurry, "Japan Earthquake Forces Thousands To Evacuate in Nuclear Plant Emergency," *The Guardian*, March 11, 2011; http://www.guardian.co.uk/world/2011/mar/11/japan-earthquake-evacuate-nuclear-plant.

[17] "The wind at last got into the clock,/The clock at last got into the wind,/The world at last got out of myself." Laura Riding, *The Poems of Laura Riding*, editor Mark Jacobs, New York: Persea, 2001 (191).

[18] Mark Epstein, *Thoughts Without a Thinker*, New York: Basic Books, 1995 (36).

[19] W.G. Sebald, *The Rings of Saturn*, Michael Husle, trans., New York: New Directions, 1998 (18).

[20] A.K.E. "Wind Turbines Grow Better Crops" in *Organic Gardening* 58:4, Jun/July 2011 (72). At blade-level though, bats and nighthawks fare badly in this Eden.

[21] The World Meteorological Organization began this practice, based on a longer standing Naval custom, in 1953.

[22] Jeff Wall, *Artist's Talk*, recording of a lecture given by the artist at the Tate Modern, London on October 25, 2005; http://www.tate.org.uk/onlineevents/archive/jeff_wall.

[23] Adapted from a speech by Robert Mitchum in *Night of the Hunter*, 1955.

[24] Theodor Adorno, *Minima Moralia: Reflections From a Damaged Life*. E.F.N. Jephcott, trans., New York: Verso, 1974 (49).

[25] This and a few other phrases throughout have been paraphrased/misremembered from the poetry of G.M. Hopkins.

Christine Hume is the author of three books, most recently *Shot* (Counterpath, 2010) and a chapbook and CD, *Lullaby: Speculations on the First Active Sense* (Ugly Duckling Presse, 2008). Lux Books in Berlin, Germany released a bilingual selected poems in 2012. She directs the interdisciplinary Creative Writing Program at Eastern Michigan University in Ypsilanti, where she lives with her partner, Jeff Clark, and their daughter, Juna.